Animals and Their
HIDING PLACES

by Jane R. McCauley

Cactus and rocks hide a cottontail and shade it from the desert sun.

BOOKS FOR YOUNG EXPLORERS
NATIONAL GEOGRAPHIC SOCIETY

Something has startled this deer. It bounds across
a stream into tall grass, where it is almost out of sight.
Then the deer keeps very still and sniffs the air.

Hiding helps animals in many ways. And animals have
different needs and different places to hide. When the cold
wind blows, the red fox finds shelter behind some grass.

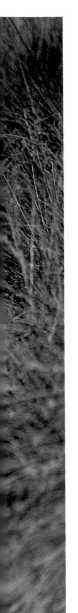

For the mountain lion, hiding is a way to catch food to eat.
This large cat uses its sharp eyes as it waits behind a log.
If a deer or other animal passes by, the cat will leap out.

While they are growing, young animals need a lot of protection. A leopard carries her cub from a tree to a safer hideaway. Like a mother house cat, she holds it gently by the neck and doesn't hurt it.

These young cheetahs sitting in the shade of a tree may be hard to find. The long, fluffy hair on their necks looks like the grass around them. When they are older, they will lose this hair. By then, they will be able to take care of themselves.

Is this bushy-tailed squirrel going to bury itself under the leaves? No, it is gathering nuts it hid there. Squirrels look for places to store food in the ground and in the trees. This chipmunk has found nuts in a tree hole. It carries them to its home in its cheek pouches, which puff out and out.

Two chipmunks meet in the tunnel leading into their burrow, or underground home. For many animals, homes are the best places to store food and to keep out of danger.

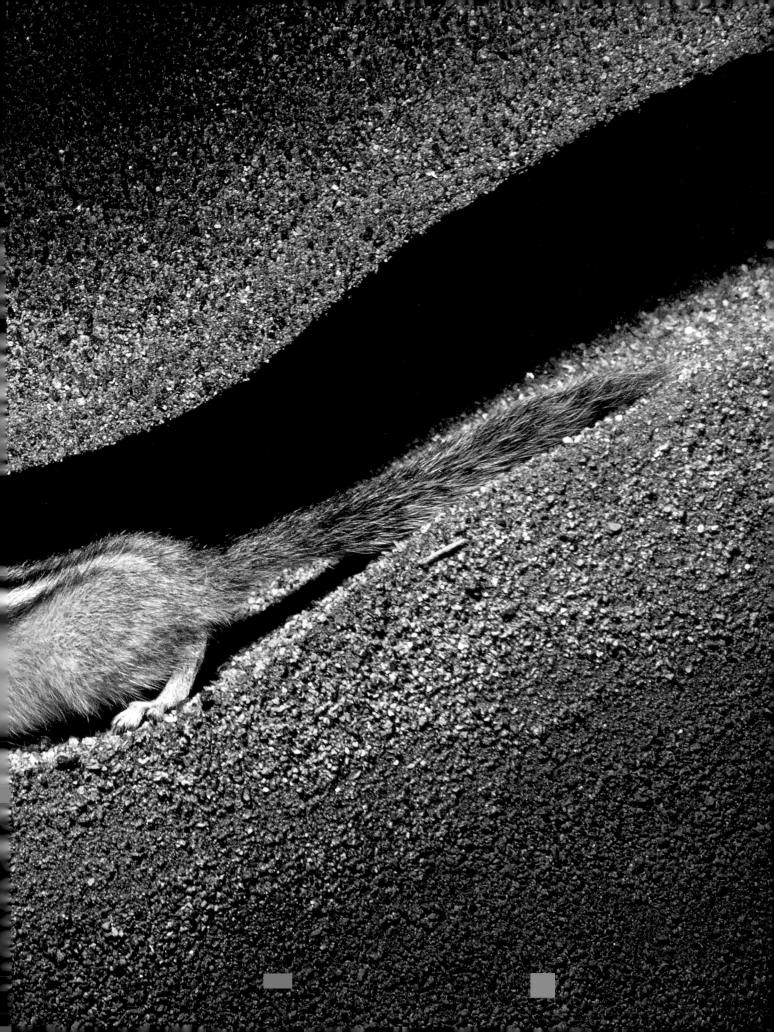

Peekaboo! A marmot pokes its head out of its den in some big rocks. If it senses danger, the marmot will slip back out of sight.

Another marmot is digging a burrow in the ground. It carries away a rock. The marmot will make more than one opening leading into its home. If an enemy comes close, the marmot can dash into the nearest hole.

Muskrats built this home in wet land called a marsh. They made the home, or lodge, from reeds in the marsh. Under the plants, a muskrat stays safe and snug. Like beavers, muskrats build the door to their home underwater. Raccoons and other animals have a hard time finding it.

Animals find safe places to live in trees, too.
A baby bluebird, eight days old, peeks out
of a tree hole. Inside, the chick stays warm and dry.
Fuzzy twigs from the nest stick to the chick's feathers.

Young bluebirds depend on their parents to bring
them food. One opens its mouth for a beetle.
Until they are old enough to fly away from danger,
bluebirds need the protection of their homes.

Golden lion tamarins hide among the leaves of a rain forest in South America. These monkeys, a little larger than squirrels, sleep in tree holes at night. The holes are often too small for other animals to get into. At dawn, the tamarins crawl from their hiding places and look for fruit and other food.

Some animals have ways to protect the soft parts of their bodies. A hermit crab pulls back inside the shell it lives in. This crab doesn't have a hard shell of its own. It lives in shells left by other animals. As it grows, it looks for a larger empty shell.

Armadillos have tough scales that help protect them. A turtle tucks itself tightly inside its hard shell.

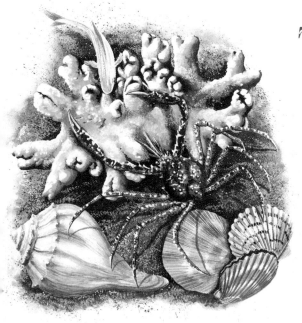

The sea urchin has long, sharp spines that keep other creatures from coming near. So why does the urchin cover itself with rocks and seashells? Maybe this is a disguise. A decorator crab also seems to hide itself. Without its disguise, the crab looks like a spider. It crawls across the rocky ocean bottom and picks up an animal called a sponge. The sponge looks like a hat on the crab!

A parrotfish hides between some rocks in a coral reef. Before it rests, it blows a clear, jellylike bubble around itself. If a hungry fish sees the parrotfish, it may not be able to reach it through the bubble. A little fish called a blenny peeks from the empty shell of another sea creature.

Blue dots brighten a ray as it rests on the bottom of the ocean. Waving its wide fins, the ray stirs up the sand and almost sinks out of sight. Soon, only its eyes show. The ray waits for other sea creatures it can catch and eat.

Like a jack-in-the-box, a jawfish pops out of its burrow in the sand. If a bigger fish swims near, the jawfish quickly pops back in.

here is the bittern? When this bird holds its head up and stretches, its striped body looks like the reeds growing in a marsh.

Because a tiny crab spider matches the color of the flower it sits on, insects it eats may not notice it. A large lion almost disappears in the tall, sandy-colored grass of an African plain.

Colors and patterns and staying out of sight help some animals keep out of danger. Hiding is perhaps the only way this fawn can protect itself until it is grown.

It is not yet strong enough to run very far. Think about places you duck into when you play a game of hide-and-seek. Would animals be safely hidden there, too?

From under a big rock, a pika keeps a careful lookout for enemies. It has piled up leaves and grasses nearby to eat during the long winter.

Cover: Curled up for a nap among the plants, a young mule deer stays very still. It might not be seen.

Published by the National Geographic Society, Washington, D. C.

Gilbert M. Grosvenor, *President*
Melvin M. Payne, *Chairman of the Board*
Owen R. Anderson, *Executive Vice President*
Robert L. Breeden, *Senior Vice President, Publications and Educational Media*

Prepared by the Special Publications Division

Donald J. Crump, *Director*
Philip B. Silcott, *Associate Director*
Bonnie S. Lawrence, *Assistant Director*

Staff for this book

Jane H. Buxton, *Managing Editor*
Karen G. Yee, *Picture Editor*
Cinda Rose, *Art Director*
Alice Jablonsky, *Researcher*
Barbara Gibson, *Artist*
Stuart E. Pfitzinger, *Illustrations Assistant*
Mary Frances Brennan, Vicki L. Broom, Carol R. Curtis, Mary Elizabeth Davis, Rosamund Garner, Virginia W. Hannasch, Artemis S. Lampathakis, Ann E. Newman, Cleo E. Petroff, Virginia A. Williams, *Staff Assistants*

Engraving, Printing, and Product Manufacture

Robert W. Messer, *Manager*
David V. Showers, *Production Manager*
George J. Zeller, Jr., *Production Project Manager*
Gregory Storer, *Senior Assistant Production Manager*
Mark R. Dunlevy, *Assistant Production Manager*
Timothy H. Ewing, *Production Assistant*

Consultants

Dr. Ine Noe, *Educational Consultant*; Dr. Lynda Bush, *Reading Consultant*
Andrew J. Baker and Dr. James M. Dietz, National Zoological Park, Smithsonian Institution; Andrew G. Gerberich, Division of Fishes, Smithsonian Institution; Carol Ann Kearns, Zoology Department, University of Maryland; Dr. Raymond B. Manning and Dr. David L. Pawson, Department of Invertebrate Zoology, Smithsonian Institution; Dr. Robert O. Petty, Professor of Biology, Wabash College; and Dr. David R. Smith, Systematic Entomology Laboratory, USDA, *Scientific Consultants*

Illustrations Credits

Bruce Dale, National Geographic Photographer (cover); John Shaw (1); Thomas Kitchin (2-3, 3 upper); Stephen J. Krasemann/Peter Arnold, Inc. (3 lower); Stephen J. Krasemann/DRK Photo (4-5); Dieter and Mary Plage/Bruce Coleman Ltd. (6-7); Masud Quraishy/Bruce Coleman Ltd. (7); Tom and Pat Leeson (8, 12 left both); Erwin and Peggy Bauer (9); Tom McHugh/National Audubon Society Collection, PR (10-11); Thomas Wiewandt (12-13); Gary R. Zahm (14-15, 28 left); Jim Brandenburg (14 lower); Michael L. Smith (16-17 both); Rod Williams/Bruce Coleman Ltd. (20 upper); Jeff Foott/Bruce Coleman Inc. (20 lower, 32); Frank Staub (21); Mark Warner (22 both); Jeff Rotman (23); Stephen Frink/WaterHouse Inc. (24-25 both); Carl Roessler (26 both, 27 lower); Russ Kinne/National Audubon Society Collection, PR (27 upper); Jen and Des Bartlett/Bruce Coleman Ltd. (28-29 lower); Ann Moreton (29 upper); Leonard Lee Rue III (30-31).

Library of Congress CIP **Data**

McCauley, Jane R., 1947-
  Animals and their hiding places.

  (Books for young explorers)
  Bibliography: p.
  Summary: Describes the various places in which animals seek safety and shelter for themselves, for their young, and for their food.
  1. Animals—Habitations—Juvenile literature. 2. Camouflage (Biology)—Juvenile literature. 3. Animal defenses—Juvenile literature. [1. Animals—Habitations. 2. Camouflage (Biology) 3. Animal defenses] I. Title. II. Series.
QL756.M35   1986   591.56′4   86-12848
ISBN 0-87044-637-1 (regular edition)   ISBN 0-87044-642-8 (library edition)

MORE ABOUT

Wherever animals live—in the desert, on mountaintops, or along the ocean bottom—hiding increases their chances for survival. To help your children understand how important hiding places are for animals, ask them if they have secret places that are special to them.

It may be helpful for children to observe a dog or cat or other household pet. Does it disappear under a couch or bed for a nap? Many kinds of animals have special places they go to for rest and safety.

On a walk in the woods, you will quickly notice that animals can stay out of sight in many ways. Some have special hiding places (10-11, 12-13, 14-15, 16-17, 18-19).* Others take cover wherever they can find it (1, 2-3, 4-5, 24-25). Some have ways of hiding themselves (22-23, 26-27). Others are camouflaged in their surroundings by their coloration or patterns.

The crab spider (29) can change color in a period of days and match different flowers. A bittern's striped body resembles the reeds of a marsh (28). And its ability to position itself upright and sway with the reeds also helps conceal it.

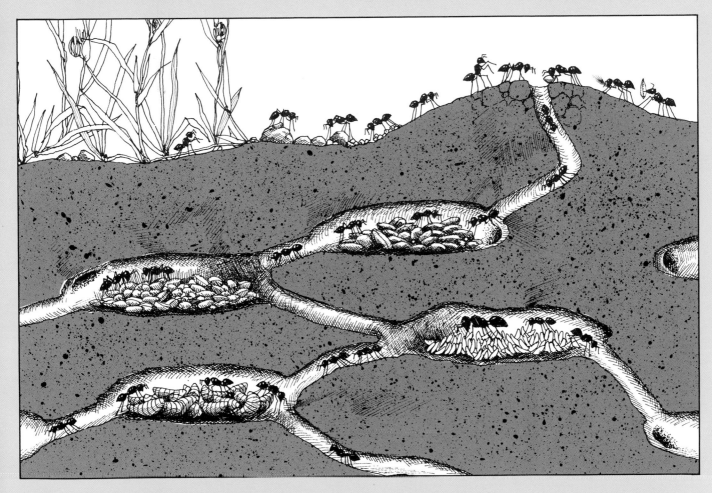

A network of tunnels links the underground hideaways of harvester ants. Chambers closest to the surface hold the unhusked and husked seeds, which serve as food for the ants. At the lower levels, nurseries shelter different stages of larvae. In building their fortresses, harvester ants hollow out passages and rooms often several feet deep in the soil. The soil they remove usually makes a mound at the entrance. Then the ants strip away the surrounding vegetation.

*Numbers in parentheses refer to pages in *Animals and Their Hiding Places*.

For vulnerable young animals, hiding is particularly important. Camouflage helps many to remain safe. As a fawn lies on the forest floor, spots on its coat may appear to be splotches of sunlight. But a fawn's camouflage seems to work only as long as it doesn't move (cover, 30-31). A mother deer keeps her baby well hidden. She also licks it daily, removing any odor that might allow other animals to track it down through smell.

A female cheetah also licks her young clean of scent. She moves them to a new hiding place every two or three days (6-7). Spotted coats and scruffy manes that look like grass enable young cheetahs to fade into their surroundings. Their camouflage is so effective that even a lion on the prowl may overlook them. Unlike fawns, which eventually lose their spotted coats, cheetahs retain their spots as adults. But their manes are gradually replaced by shorter, coarser hair.

For most animals, the best refuge for offspring is their home. Bluebirds (16-17) use tree holes as safe nurseries for their helpless babies. Once abundant, bluebirds have dwindled in number as trees have been felled for urban expansion.

Loss of trees has also caused the decline of golden lion tamarins (18-19). Today only about 400 of these monkeys survive in the rain forests of Brazil. There, they stay behind the thick leaves and vines of the jungle canopy by day. At night, an entire family will crowd into a deep tree hole. Tamarins do not have to climb down to the ground for food. They find lizards, small frogs, and insects living in small pools of water that collect in bromeliads, plants that grow along the tree trunks.

A number of animals build homes that are especially good fortresses against predators. The muskrat (14-15) constructs its dome-shaped lodge in marshy areas from mud and plants, often forming a moat around it. Though easily visible, the lodge deters most predators because its only access lies underwater. Inside their dwelling, muskrats sleep and raise their young in various rooms above the water level.

In some places, muskrats dig burrows along the banks of rivers and streams instead of building a lodge. Muskrats also make temporary shelters, safe places where they can climb out of the water to eat rather than returning to a burrow or lodge.

Like land animals, sea creatures rely on hiding for defense and to capture food. Moray eels, parrotfish (24-25), and blennies (25) are among those that seek sanctuary in the dark recesses of a coral reef. Since as many as 400 species of fish may thrive on a reef, competition for food is keen.

Decorator crabs (23) mask themselves with seaweed or pieces of live sponges. More baffling are sea urchins (22). Though they can inflict injury with their sharp spines, they still cover themselves with rocks and seashells. Scientists speculate that this behavior may protect them from sunlight or from birds that might snatch them at low tide.

It is difficult to explore reef life without special equipment. But you and your children can learn a lot about the hiding behavior of animals by observing those near your home. Be patient, however, for animals have niches where they can keep away from intruders. These activities may help you in your search:

• Go on several hikes in the woods, keeping a record of the animals you discover. Where do they go to get away? Listen to the sounds around you, and try to pick out where they are coming from. In the fall, look for squirrels or chipmunks storing food. Remember to leave the woods as you find it. Talk to your children about the importance of not disturbing animals' homes.

• A raccoon has discovered a muskrat lodge. Invite your child to make up a story about the muskrats inside their home. Look back at page 14 before you begin. Will the raccoon find the entrance to the lodge?

• Would your child like to have a pet hermit crab? Many pet stores sell land hermit crabs. You will need a glass terrarium or goldfish bowl. Put a layer of sand about three inches deep in it, and add some rocks and branches for the crab to climb on. Cover the terrarium with fine wire mesh if the crab can climb out. Keep it out of direct sunlight.

Hermit crabs will eat many of the same things you do. In the evening, feed them bites of meat and apple, lettuce, and carrots organically grown or scrubbed to remove pesticides. Don't forget that your pet will need several different shells to wear as it grows. Keep its home free of uneaten food. Before buying a hermit crab, learn more about it by reading some books in your library.

ADDITIONAL READING

Fun With Land Hermit Crabs, by Daniele Scermino. (St. Petersburg, Fl., Palmetto Publishing Co., 1978). Ages 8 and up.

Gadabouts and Stick-at-Homes, by Lorus and Margery Milne. (N.Y., Sierra Club Books/Charles Scribner's Sons, 1980). Ages 9 and up.

How Animals Defend Their Young, by Russell Freedman. (N.Y., E.P. Dutton, 1978). Ages 10 and up.

Protective Coloration and Mimicry, ed. by Roger Caras. (Richmond, Va., Westover Publishing Co., 1972). Ages 10 and up.